a

ONE HEART
DIVERSE MIND

The Quaker Universalist Way

Adrian Cairns

QUAKER HOME SERVICE
•London•

First published in December 1994
by Quaker Home Service

ISBN   0 85245 263 2

Contents

Preface

In March, 1993, some dozen members of the Quaker Universalist Group's Committee gathered for a week-end retreat at Turvey Abbey in Bedfordshire. Their object was to take time to consider in an un-pressured way the *raison d'etre* of the group, and to suggest its likely future course. Towards this end, each member was asked to produce a short paper beforehand, outlining their personal understanding and recommendations for discussion. These 'Turvey Papers' were made available to the Annual Conference in April 1993 for comment, for it was always the aim of the Committee to be seen as servants of the membership, not its directors. The papers and comments have now provided source-material among others mentioned in the present essay, and I am very grateful to the various Friends mentioned in the 'Notes' for permission to quote their words, often out of their original context, and sometimes in support of a point whose expression has been my sole responsibility; as, indeed, has been the inclusion of later material referring to events in 1994.

1 What is a Quaker Universalist ?

'Universal' is a large and many-faceted word for a simple idea. Jane Austen uses it with delicious hyperbole in the first sentence of *Pride and Prejudice* when she suggests that 'It is a truth universally acknowledged that a single man in possession of a good fortune, must be in want of a wife.' My dictionary offers a prime definition of this usage as meaning 'extends over, comprehends, affects or includes the whole of something specified or implied'. A secondary definition is obviously that which is 'of or throughout the universe', but this may also be allowed to mean only 'of the world or all nature' or even simply 'existing or occurring everywhere or in all things'. The dictionary goes on to define it in relation to law, to language, to logic and philosophy, to the Church, to persons, to machines, to arithmetic and to suffrage. The word is clearly overloaded with separate meanings according to where it finds itself.

So what about 'Universalism' and 'Universalist'? Here the *Shorter Oxford Dictionary* is much less forthcoming. Theologically, Universalism refers to the doctrine of universal salvation or redemption, or the belief that all people will be saved regardless of circumstance; and a Universalist is one who believes in this, or in the United States is specifically 'a member of a sect holding this doctrine'. *Chambers Dictionary of Beliefs and Religions* goes on to say that Universalism 'implies rejection of the traditional Christian belief in hell', and that it is 'a feature of much contemporary Protestant theology' which is motivated by 'a recognition of the validity of other non-Christian world faiths'. The latter is about the only point where a dictionary definition even begins to approach the meaning of the word in its present context.

What, then, is a Quaker Universalist? (This is not yet defined at all in the *Oxford Dictionary*, but the omission is in the process

of being corrected.) In view of the universalist ideas propound-
ed by William Penn and other early Quakers - for example,
Penn's unambiguous tenet about devout souls being 'everywhere of one religion' - it is quite surprising to note the term
is quite recent. It was probably first used by John Linton in a
talk given to the Seekers Association in 1977 called *Quakerism
as Forerunner*. In this he spoke of 'a universalist point of view'
and 'the universalism of the Quaker message' and how Quakerism should 'move towards a universalist position'. Christianity
he saw, and sees, as too 'parochial', but for those who 'still want
to follow Jesus... that is still within a universal framework'. That
was the start of the movement and the Group. Since its inception
following John Linton's talk, the Quaker Universalist Group
(henceforward referred to as the QUG) has been very fortunate
in having the scholarly and passionate support of Ralph Hetherington. In the summer of 1993 he had a pamphlet published,
Universalism and Spirituality [1], in which he notes three major
'defining marks of Quaker Universalism' as:
(i) *The Reality of the Inward Light*, which reflects '...the possibil-
ity of a direct, unmediated communication between the individual
human being and the creative source of love, light and life for
which we commonly use the term God.';
(ii) *The Primacy of the Inward Light over Scripture*; and
(iii) *The Belief in 'That of God' in Everyone*; which rejects the
Augustinian teaching of original sin with its Fall and Redemption
theology. Quaker Universalists, believing in '...no unbridgeable
gap between God and human beings', are more compatible with
what is called today 'creation-centred spirituality'.

There seems nothing in Hetherington's 'defining marks'
which most Quakers would not accept, so where, precisely, are
the differences in being a Quaker Universalist? Before I came
to Quakers some fourteen years ago, I was fearful of acceptance by a group reputedly so principled and strict in their ways.
Indeed, I found them so; yet they also had such a warm and

liberally open-minded attitude to 'free-thinkers' like myself that, like so many before me, I felt I had arrived at my spiritual 'home'. The overtly Christian language and wide biblical scholarship evident among some Elders and others, and in the *Book of Discipline*, remained rather daunting; but I soon recognized that alongside this was an honesty about contemporary experience and an individual integrity of spiritual searching which more than balanced the discomfort of what I felt was an outmoded theology. Shortly, I was introduced to the *Universalist* magazine and the QUG. The main difference between being a Quaker and a Quaker Universalist struck me as residing in this business of accepting the diversity of liveries which make us strangers, and that 'when death has taken off the mask' we would all know each other. Penn has always spoken to my condition rather more than Fox, and while we are clearly all of one heart, whether as Quakers or anyone else, some Quaker minds are more diverse than others. The breadth of diversity exemplified in the QUG with its insistence on spiritual awareness being accessible to all without exclusive conditions, seemed to me very special within the one Society of Friends of the Truth, as I found we originally called ourselves.

The main difference, in brief, between a Quaker and a Quaker Universalist is the vital emphasis placed by the latter on the universalist roots of the Society. In a similar fashion, the American Quaker Universalist Fellowship describe themselves as, 'Friends and others influenced by the strains of Quaker thought that warn against literalism and celebrate the universality of inward religious experience.'

Hetherington's pamphlet takes his reader through these historical roots of universalist ideas in Quakerism, from the aforementioned Penn and his concept of pagan spirituality whereby the Inward Light 'lighteth every man that cometh into the world', through Penington and Fox and Barclay, then to Elias Hicks in America in 1827, and the Manchester Conference in

1895 which 'made biblical criticism respectable and freed Quakers from a constricting fundamentalism'. Worldwide Friends remain divided over the actual primacy of the Inward Light over scripture; but universalists are firmly with those who believe in the Esoteric Tradition, sometimes called the Perennial Philosophy, as it reveals its historical continuity in the mystical basis of Quakerism, so pertinently researched by Rufus Jones. Jones, incidentally, once noted in true universalist fashion that 'Religion is an experience which no definition exhausts.' Hetherington concludes that Quaker Universalism is particularly well fitted to answer such contemporary needs as the urgency for current international recognition of 'green issues' and the protection of the ecosphere as part of a spiritual as well as material cosmos in which all creation is interdependent. It is, in fact, quite an old idea whose time has not only come into its own at last, but which carries with it the hope of helping to safeguard our threatened future.

Friends in Britain, it has seemed to me from some of their writings, are increasingly expressing the necessity of dragging Quakerism into the twenty-first century with a change of emphasis in its theology. It is no accident that, for example, Rex Ambler, lecturer in theology at Birmingham University, can give seven affirmations of what Quakerism stands for without once mentioning Jesus or Christianity.[2] It is symptomatic of the 'movement' or 'process' taking place in the Society. In the old *Advices and Queries* there were eight mentions of Jesus and eighteen of Christ or Christianity; the newly-accepted re-draft has only four and six, respectively. At Yearly Meeting, 1994, as it was struggling with the birth pangs of the new *Book of Discipline*, mental anguish was expressed by some over such omissions and the absence of reference to elements of traditional Christianity such as the resurrection. But the uncomfortable truth is that 'pain' (as it is more often referred to by Friends) is the inevitable consequence of change, of growth, and of evolving maturity, in theology as in everything else. There is also 'pain' experienced by others, or at any rate, mental discomfort, at the rigidity enforced by old forms and old language resisting change, and stunting growth. The 'offence' taken by some Friends is an 'offence' given to others. There is no escaping this equation; life is like that; and the suffering entailed must be endured, with understanding and patience, from either side of the balance. As Yearly Meeting made tenderly clear, some passions - from whatever quarter - have to be 'set aside' for the general 'sense of the meeting' in 'seeking the right way forward'.

Nevertheless, in answer to the increasing pace of change, often spearheaded (forgive the old phrase!) by those with universalist attitudes, it has to be observed that there is currently a defensive and conservative wave of traditional Christian witness, among Quakers as among other branches of a beleaguered Christian Church, wishing to maintain the status quo. But equally observable is the rising tide of fresh and courageous thinking, even among clergy, seeking to recreate more honestly our individual, unmediated relationships with the Divine. A *cause célèbre* in the summer of 1994 dramatically illustrates this dichotomy.

2 The post-Christian 'God-as-it-were'

Ten years ago, in 1984, BBC television transmitted a series of programmes called *The Sea of Faith* presented by the then Dean of Emmanuel College, Cambridge, the Rev Don Cupitt. The series took its title from Matthew Arnold's poem *Dover Beach*, written in the 1860's and giving an unforgettable image for what the poet saw as the decline of religion in his time:

The Sea of Faith
Was once, too, at the full, and round earth's shore
Lay like the folds of a bright girdle furled.
But now I only hear its melancholy, long, withdrawing roar,
Retreating, to the breath
Of the night-wind, down the vast edges drear
And naked shingles of the world.

Five years later in 1989, a Sea of Faith Network was formed to pursue Cupitt's ideas of a post-Christian religious faith, located firmly in this world, entirely human, limited by language, yet centred in spiritual and caring activity. He himself was never the 'leader' of the group, though he attends its conferences and writes for its quarterly magazine when he can. The Sea of Faith Network has a very mixed membership from Humanist to Roman Catholic, with Anglicans perhaps dominating among a minority of clergymen, but heavily outnumbered by non-clerics and agnostics. Its six hundred or so members includes some Quakers, and especially Quaker Universalists, because, as one of their spokesmen, David Boulton, says: 'By its nature, Sea of Faith is universalist.' In its liberating way, without creed or involvement with any institutionalized religion, it is for a number of priests much the same as the QUG is for the Religious Society of Friends. It is in the *avant-garde*; and quite possibly may become the main voice in a post-Christian twenty-first century when its heretical messages pass into orthodoxy, and metaphor and symbol are seen to carry more significance than 'literal' truth. Much the same might be said of Quaker Universalism.

That 'long, withdrawing roar' of institutionalized faith is still rumbling in 1994. It is sometimes called 'Churchianity' to distinguish it from the true Christianity which, as G K Chesterton observed, has hardly been tried yet. The roar has seldom been so obvious as in the case of the Rev Anthony Freeman: even his name is symbolic! Mr Freeman was the priest-in-charge at St Mark's in the small, rural village of Staplefield in West Sussex. In 1993, as an ironic fate would have it, he was invited to write a short book telling the story of his personal spiritual journey as a way of helping spread the gospel. That book, called *God in Us: A Case for Christian Humanism*, spoke of God as having no external existence, but being rather the creation of the human heart and mind, a sum-total of all that was good in the world. 'There is nothing out there,' he wrote, 'or, if there is, we can have no knowledge of it.' Not an exceptional view among Quaker Universalists, although obviously posing some difficulties of conscience and the use of language for a practising priest. Mr Freeman's bishop was a leading Anglo-Catholic and bastion of the traditional Church, so that when he read the book, it inevitably shocked him. After consultation with his peers and others, Dr. Eric Kemp, Bishop of Chichester, dismissed Mr Freeman from his post as director of post-ordination training, and gave him a year to consider his future at St Mark's. That year soon passed during which Mr Freeman could not find it in his conscience to recant. As a result, he became the first Anglican priest in this century to be dismissed for publishing unorthodox views.

It caused quite a furore. Sixty-five fellow ministers, including Don Cupitt, Paul Oestreicher and Keith Ward, put their names to a letter in *The Independent* calling the occasion of Mr

Freeman's last official sermon, 'a day of sorrow for those who value breadth and openness.' For over a week, the nation's press and letters columns, and the radio and television networks, had a field-day with headings like 'A priest who pushed dissent too far', 'So what is God really like?' and '"unbeliver priest" defiant to the end'. It was all rather predictable; and the only reason for it all was that a sincere, honest, unsophisticated, conscience-stricken priest had used lay language to state the obvious about the most profound of theological issues, and especially about the nature and existence - or non-objective existence - of God.   Mr Freeman had quite mildly pointed out that the Emperor had no clothes. The same observation, or at any rate, the same intellectual attitude, coming as it has done frequently before from the austere eyries of Oxbridge would seem to concern no one in the media.

In David Hare's fine play *Racing Demon*, about the state of the Church of England today, the beleaguered inner city priest, the Rev Lionel Espy, is obliged to coin the phrase 'God-as-it-were' to avoid putting off his street-wise and cynical congregation. If 'God-as-it-were' is ever to become a national issue, clearly He must do it on the media's terms; any Second Coming would have to pass the test of tabloid headlines before the Vatican even got near it; or as the popular scientist, Bryan Appleyard, put it: 'Unless He can come up with something big, God is on the way out.'[3] I do not think that is true. As has been said before, if God did not exist, it would be necessary to create Him - as, indeed, has always been done. We simply have to go on doing it in a more acceptable way, given the historical advances in knowledge about ourselves, our consciousness, and the universe around us.

The Rev Freeman, as it happens, is one of the minority of Anglican priests who are members of the Sea of Faith Network. It is reported that many, even hundreds, outside the network support his views, albeit surreptitiously for fear of offending not only their bishop but their more conservative parishioners, and of course for fear of their livings. Mr Freeman, in this respect, has unwillingly been given the role of martyr; although he has not carried it at all tragically but with humour and grace. His story has been a dramatic rite of passage - moving into, through, and out of the official Church. Just a day or two before he gave his farewell sermon to the parishioners of St Mark's he was attending the Sea of Faith Conference at Leicester University where I was involved with him in a small group workshop concerned with 'Creating Rites of Passage'. He was the obvious subject for some practical work, so in silent mime the group told his story, briefly and simply. It was an emotional event, and even - I think it might be hazarded - redolent of conciliation and healing. Only a few days later, the small private 'ritual farewell' so clearly enacted for the Conference was almost exactly duplicated on the TV screens of the nation. Mr Freeman bade farewell to his parishioners at his church door, embracing each in turn. It was an important demonstration of the power of symbolic action, of the truth as shadow matching the truth as real; and I mention it in some detail here as an illustration, because in the conclusion to this essay, I point to how Quaker Universalism might express itself in action, and perhaps develop a living theology through the use of art-forms.

3 Global consciousness and ongoing process

The Green movement as a contemporary issue is a reminder that so-called primitive races may have got more things right than modern thinking gives credit. They understood the totality of Nature and their place in it. Primal religions, or 'native spiritualities', need to be looked at again. 'They lived in balance and reverence with the natural world, and we do not.'[4] Matthew Fox, of *Original Blessing* fame, uses a special technical term for the concept of 'God being in all things and all things being in God'. It is *panentheism*, which is subtly different from *pantheism*. Pantheism is defined as 'God being everything and everything being God' and hence describing the heathen worship of all the many gods which are given names. With panentheism, on the other hand, 'Divinity is not outside us. We are in God and God is in us. That is the unitive experience of the mystics East and West.'[5] Now, our new scientific understanding, especially through the implications of quantum theory and the rapid growth of 'global consciousness', is pointing again to that total interconnectedness and dependence of all things which was mentioned earlier. This new knowledge, essentially universalist, does not seek to detract from the 'distinctiveness' of expression in each great religion. It is of an inclusive and not exclusive nature, as we shall be discussing more fully later. We have to admit, for all our advances, that we are not necessarily *wiser* than previous ages; we merely *know* a lot more about the material universe. Another American theologian tells us that 'we must rediscover the dimensions of consciousness of the spirituality of the primal peoples' and that 'this new global consciousness must be organically ecological, supported by structures that will ensure justice and peace'.[6]

Creation, which must include what we call 'God', is an ongoing process, a force working towards wholeness and harmony, and whose mystery we can only touch at different levels of our being. We ourselves, our bodies and personalities, are but formw of that creation; and we also create our own forms, not only in the arts, but in religions and institutions; yet in the final analysis, 'all forms are temporary and will die'. This makes it an uncertain world, and because we can only bear a limited uncertainty, we are doomed to failure in our religious guesses where 'All "certainties" are a defence against the greater reality.'[7] The 'security' of fundamentalism can be no more than a temporary anodyne, destined to ultimately fail and disappoint. The greater reality cannot be born easily. It challenges a responsibility which only great courage, suffering and love can meet. It is not at all comfortable, as witness the recorded agonies of the saints and mystics struggling with the dark night of their souls. But it can also be the supreme prize, hard won, beyond pride and even personal possession; for there can be no ego present, no self that is not every self, no separate identity from the total identity of an absolute consciousness, where all is light and joy and compassion and understanding, and that incredible power and ultimate security we call love.

The second part of Yearly Meeting in 1994 was much exercised at one stage with an addition to the new *Book of Discipline* by Sidney Bailey which concluded: 'Peace is a process to engage in, not a goal to be reached.' Perhaps those friends who were worried by this statement might have found some illumination from Thich Nhat Hanh, the Vietnamese meditation master, who once wrote that 'There is no way to peace. Peace is the way.' It is much the same with our concepts of God: there is no way to Him. He is the way. It is said that the Church only exists to pursue the establishment of God's Kingdom on earth. If that goal is ever reached then there would seem to be no further need for the Church. We could get rid of it. Karen Armstrong commented as much on Radio 4's 'Moral Maze' when it was discussing conscience and the Anthony Freeman case.

Moreover, if God is a presence with us now, again there would seem no need for an intermediary priesthood. Quakers, especially, understand that; and Quaker Universalists, perhaps, more than most. It would appear that the time has already come to call in the bluff of St Paul's creation, the Church, with all its unnecessarily invested power. As Karen Armstrong concludes in her much-acclaimed book *A History of God*, 'The idols of fundamentalism are not good substitutes for God; if we are to create a vibrant new faith for the twenty-first century, we should, perhaps, ponder the history of God for some lessons and warnings.'[8]

Universalism is not about God or substitutes for God, nor about opposites, the division of one against another; it is not even about right and wrong, good and bad, the contention of ideas and arguments. It is about harmony, about the music of the heavenly spheres and the separate chords of sunrise and cloud-set, the oneness of desert and flood, fire and ice. It is about the wholeness of Nature, and of our part in it.

Or if that is rather too poetic for some tastes, let us look at an academic's view of universalism. Rex Ambler, mentioned earlier and who is a Quaker, sees his subject as one which is there 'to illuminate and not to stipulate'. We need to articulate a global spirituality, he says, and to share our understandings rather than our dogmas. This is a most encouraging attitude which is in keeping with much contemporary thinking across the spectrum of churches and faiths which recognize a form of universalism. Ambler sees it as 'a universalism of potential, since what it affirms is the potential of all human beings to realize their unity with other human beings, and with them a unity with God'.[9] It does not claim 'that actual religious experiences will always be essentially the same', but rather that the very differences help a better understanding of our mutual human situation through dialogue between each other. He also sees other interpretations of universalism affecting inter-faith relations, and incidentally, what he suggests is the 'misunder-standing' of Quakers concerning 'Christocentric' and 'Universalist' viewpoints. His first 'most cautious interpretation' is the same as the QUG's assertion that 'spiritual awareness (he calls it 'true religious experience') is accessible to men and women of any religion or none... ' His second interpretation sees this experi-ence, or awareness, as the essential 'core' of every religion, however disguised or distorted by cultural and historical factors. Thirdly, this 'primary expression' may be seen as the same, or universal, in every religion; and fourthly, the dictionary definition already quoted whereby everyone will be 'saved' whatever their mode of spiritual consciousness. In universalism, so to speak, 'all paths lead to God'. Only the third of these interpretations will offer difficulties to the Christocentric Quaker. The dogmatic statement in John 14.6 about Jesus saying that 'no one comes to the Father except by me' is a 'particularity' which cannot be shared. Ambler also comments that in reasoning about the spiritual life, we have to admit, at every step, the inadequacy of words; and at the same time, their indispensability. To articulate our beliefs may not, at the last stage of experience, be actually possible in words; but the attempt to do so may not only be necessary but beneficial. To suppress internal conflicts and uncertainties, instead of trying to work them out through dia-logue, may well prove spiritually unhealthy.

Sensing this danger, there is a need, even a desperate one in some quarters for a forum in which those of a universal-ist turn of mind can meet and discuss and share their stumbling apprehension of these things. The Quaker mode of meeting for worship provides an extremely valuable basis and focus out of which the pursuit of such a forum can take place. The Quaker movement has a vital role in this respect, furthering 'new ways of expressing old truths', helping to 'push out the boundaries with new enlightenment in new language', being at once a cutting-edge for the advance of spiritual consciousness and the growing point of its own destiny. But should such an analysis seem too cold and intellectual, we must never forget the prime commandment, which comes before and after all fabrications of thought and institutionalized concepts - the simple, unequivocal command to love one another.[10]

The 'misunderstanding' between so-called 'Christocentric' and 'Universalist' viewpoints, referred to by Ambler, has found a happy resolvement in a fresh addition to Chapter 28 of our new *Book of Discipline*. It is a joint statement by parties of each and neither persuasion which reads:

> We have acquired a much greater understanding of non-Christian religions from newcomers who have settled in this country since the end of World War II and this has increased the sympathy and respect of many Friends for these faiths. This broader approach to religion has led to an affirmation by 'universalist' Friends that no one faith can claim to be a final revelation or to have a monopoly of the truth and to the rejection of any exclusive religious fundamentalism whether based in Christianity or any other religion.

> The ferment of thought in this post-war period has produced a wide variety of beliefs in our Religious Society today and not a little misunderstanding on all sides. Intolerance has reared its head. Some Friends have voiced objections to the use of Christian language in meetings for worship and for business; others have been told that there is no place for them in our Religious Society if they cannot regard themselves as Christians. It has become quite customary to distinguish between 'Christians' and 'universalists' as if one category excluded the other.

> This situation has led many Friends to suppose that universalist Friends are in some way set over against Christocentric Friends. This is certainly not the case. Universalism is by definition inclusivist, and its adherents accept the right to free

definition inclusivist, and its adherents accept the right to free expression of all points of view, Christocentric or any other. Indeed, in (Britain) Yearly Meeting there are many universalists whose spiritual imagery and belief are thoroughly Christocentric.

From the beginning the Quaker Christian faith has had a universal dimension. George Fox saw the Light 'shine through all' and he identified it with the divine Light of Christ that 'enlightens every man that comes into the world' (John, I:9). He pointed out, as did William Penn in greater detail, that individuals who had lived before the Christian era or outside Christendom and had no knowledge of the Bible story, had responded to a divine principle within them. In these terms, all Quaker Christians are universalists. Obedience to the Light within, however that may be described, is the real test of faithful living.

Alastair Heron, Ralph Hetherington
and Joseph Pickvance, 1994.

As with the three signatories to this joint declaration, the true universalism will be when thinkers of all persuasions may find it possible, through love and mutual respect, to come and meet together in their differences. They may not achieve a common understanding through a shared terminology - that is most unlikely - but at least they will have acknowledged their common feelings and their common humanity.[11]

4 Quaker Universalism is inclusive not exclusive

We can never really know which of our words will resonate with others far beyond their original context. What would George Fox and, to take another example, Shakespeare, have made of the fact that several hundred years later, some of their most casual words, often only part of a longer phrase, achieved such prime significance? 'Be patterns... and come to walk cheerfully...' 'To be or not to be...' 'Be still and cool in thy own mind and spirit...' 'Out, out brief candle! Life's but a walking shadow...' and '...What canst thou say?' These are words which touch a common nerve in us all.

It was one such phrase with which John Linton, the founder of Quaker Universalism, first expounded his case. In his seminal talk to The Seekers' Association in 1977 he said that he liked to think that Quakerism is about the search for Truth and that 'Truth is wider than Christianity'. That led him to 'the universalist position' which he saw should be completely detached from indoctrination, a process to which most of the human race is exposed from its earliest years. Was it possible to be a 'religious rationalist' whilst knowing that 'religion goes beyond reason'? The universalist would probably think so, because the religious impulse in all members of the human race may be rationally perceived as either leading to delusion or enlightenment, but only experientially can the difference be decided.

There are some Friends, as is frequently shown in the letter pages of *The Friend*, for whom so-called Quaker 'fringe groups' are divisive. They are seen as 'watering down' the 'true faith' and 'Quaker morality' and encouraging a frivolous acceptance of 'anything goes' in the experiential truth of individual members. This is to misconceive what has been described as 'a sign of vitality within our Yearly Meeting'.[12] Far from being an 'anything goes religion', modern Quakerism is more inclined to insist on being a 'nothing goes religion which does not owe obedience to the Inward Light' whatever form such obedience may take. Whatever our concept of 'God' may be, it is a hard and not a weak task-creator. The priorities, so rightly given by Jesus, are that the concept should be loved with all our being, and that because of it we should behave to others as we would have them behave to us. There is no weakening of morality there.

The role of the QUG is precisely to emphasize inclusivity rather than exclusivity, a role which has always been the special contribution of heretical Quakerism in challenging the officially established viewpoint. Quaker Universalism, as we have already seen from the joint statement, is wrongly seen by some as being in opposition to Christocentric views; and by those who think it *is* in opposition, it is often 'rubbished' as being obvious and lacking in depth of thought. The fact is, as was mentioned earlier, that inclusivity focuses uncomfortably on Christianity's own specific dilemma: namely that it can only be inclusive of other religious traditions by contradicting its own belief in particularity. But this dilemma has never been apparent in the same way in the mystical strands of Christianity, of which Quakerism is often quoted as one. In these, the Christ figure is often seen in his cosmic spiritual dimension, 'open to humankind from the beginning and not limited in time or place'. This is the early Quaker inheritance and understanding of the Christian faith. As such, it may well continue to stand in its rebellious way at 'the forefront of the religious search for universal reconciliation'.[13]

The inclusivist nature of Universalism, of course, embraces not only those of Christian persuasion but also includes the Hindu, the Buddhist, the Muslim and so on, not forgetting the Humanist agnostic. The point about universalist spirituality is in the belonging, whatever mode it takes. As Thomas Merton said, 'To be religious and serious about it one must, generally, belong to a religion.' We need our religious roots, in most cases, as we need our linguistic and cultural ones. It is only through being thus connected that we can respond sensitively to the deepest elements in another. Merton was a prime example of one whose own deep commitment enabled him to build what might be called 'universalist bridges' between Christianity and the Taoist, Buddhist and Hindu faiths. 'One of the signs of our time', it has been said, 'is that the world religions can no longer live in isolation from each other.'[14] Fundamentalism in any of them tends to deaden their spirituality.

Universalists are sometimes derided for being syncretic, that is, for aiming to reconcile and unify different traditions. But that is not the case at all, even if it were possible. The Quaker Universalist would wish to preserve intact the separate diversities of religious faith whilst taking an overall view. Moreover, past history shows that so called unique traditions have invariably expropriated and absorbed to themselves anything usefully rooted around them. 'New' forms have often grown out of pre-existent ones which were given re-definition. This is not syncretism. No more are Quaker Universalists syncretic in moving towards the vision of a global spirituality, seeking to express a convergent yet always emergent faith; one which acknowledges what Lorna Marsden has called 'the universality of the image'[15] which underpins all religions, yet also acknowledging its specific expression in different vocabularies. As has been established, it is no part of the Quaker Universalist way to be intolerant of Christian vocabulary, or any other, in the expression of faith. On the other hand, an intolerant dogmatism from whatever quarter has no part in its philosophy either.

It has been suggested that Universalists are people who have reacted against the strictures and hypocrisies often present in a Christian upbringing. That may be an element in some cases, but it is certainly not a pre-requisite for being a Universalist. The reverse, rather, is the case. Those who are intolerant of Christian language, as of any other, are *not* following a Universalist position. Tolerance is an important factor which is often misunderstood by those who can only see it as a weakness. It is, in fact, a great strength and a saving grace for any religious organization which hopes to meet the challenges of today's world. It is the antidote to fossilization and the rigidities of fundamentalism, and an attitude which deserves to be celebrated. It allows for 'creative listening' and a compassionate understanding - not necessarily agreement - with those of different persuasions. This openness, however, does not extend to the blinkered activities of bodies like the Evangelical Alliance. Such unquestioning 'certainty' and exclusivity can only be a retrogressive factor in the building of 'universalist bridges'.

Being a Quaker in the 20th century is surely ultimately defined by our concept of the Inward Light as an individual manifestation. That Light is a *continuing* revelation in which truth occurs as process. Nothing is fixed. There is no final answer, no 'theory of everything' as some scientists are hoping shortly to achieve. We are not here in a mathematical field where it may prove possible. We are not even in a spatio-temporal one. The essential mystery at the heart of things resides in untold dimensions beyond our very limited capacity to understand in this life. Yet this life is surely all there is, at least for us. This world, in some extraordinary way, is it. To echo the heretical thoughts of Anthony Freeman, there is no other stage of which we can be aware on which the creative consciousness, the Logos, is unfolding its cosmic drama.

5 Literal or metaphorical:
What canst thou say ?

John Hick, editor of that seminal book of the Seventies, *The Myth of God Incarnate*, has identified Christianity's current crisis as having 'to decide whether it is literal or metaphorical'. He was also one of those who wrote to *The Independent* about the 'vulnerable' Mr Freeman, but making the point that it is not a case of God being *either* a sort of 'cosmic Father Christmas' *or* simply a 'purely human projection'. More subtly, he opts for a 'critical realist' attitude rather than the 'anti-realism' of Cupitt, and before him, of Ludwig Feuerbach in the early 19th century. There is certainly nothing new in all this discussion; and in Christian terms, Hick sees God as 'an ultimate transcendent Reality... benign in relation to human life... humanly reflected ("incarnated") in the lives of the world's great spiritual leaders'... among whom Jesus can be found as a principal revelation and guide.[16] Most Universalists would not argue with that although for Quaoers generally, it has mostly seemed non-productive to worry about these 'faith issues' in such an intellectual way. They prefer to address the priorities of social concern and service. They already 'know' a firm basis in their regard for silent worship, where what they 'believe' does not have to be articulated. They have a mistrust of scripture and language generally, and are more readily persuaded that behaviour speaks louder than proclamation. 'By your actions are you known.' Quaker Universalists, of course, concur with this. Where they get more worried than the average Quaker is in squaring their intellectual conscience when dealing with some of the elementary tenets expected of Christians. Even some bishops have been uncomfortably exercised over this, wishing to see an end to the 'literalist' interpretation of events such as the 'virgin birth', the miracles which are contrary to natural law (though the 'healing miracles' may simply be beyond current medical understanding), and any suggestion of a physical 'ascension into the clouds.' On the whole these things speak symbolically or by metaphor, unlike the direct wisdom of the parables and much of the Sermon on the Mount. But for all this, Universalist Friends would probably recognize that there is a false dichotomy in separating the dimensions of spirit and matter which partake of one substance and existential reality. In this regard, one Friend has asked whether it is not time to 'reject altogether the dualism of the supernatural'.[17]

But in pursuing such ideals, we must not forget the 'other side' of our human nature. C G Jung reminds that '...none of us stands outside humanity's black collective shadow... We are in a split condition to begin with... and recognition of the shadow leads to the modesty we need in order to acknowledge imperfection.' Too often, we cloak our inner world with deceptive language, when the real point is to ask 'exactly how ideal themselves are people who talk of ideals?' 'To counter this danger,' says Jung, 'the free society needs a bond of an affective nature, a principle of a kind like *caritas*, the Christian love of your neighbour.'[18] We will be returning to that.

Both 'God' and 'Christianity' in history may be seen very differently from the 'dark' angle of observation. Would an all-powerful creator really subscribe to man's centuries of vileness by staying at one remove, leaving us to infer either that he couldn't interfere with free will or just didn't care? Also, Christianity's evolvement has been a manifest failure of a supposedly omnipotent will. A Friend writes that

> Two thousand years may be a blink in the experience of the Almighty, but it's a hell of a long time for suffering humanity. To send one's son, or a projection of oneself, to "save" the world, on this basis, was a pretty lamentable operation in the first place (on the human level we would call it sadism or sadomasochism), and in the event, the Church got the message wrong. Think of all the wars that would have been avoided if it had eschewed slaughter over the centuries![19]

There is an undeniable honesty behind this comment. Will Christianity, or rather, more accurately, 'churchianity' - the whole man-made, male-orientated, theological and credal edifice which is supposed to be guiding our sinful natures towards salvation - will it ever be able to admit that 'it got it wrong' - not so much about Jesus and what he taught, nor even about the Cosmic Christ or Spirit that is with us always - but over Pauline theology and the construction and manipulation of creeds and language (not to mention translations) centuries after the event? The latest encyclical to come out of Rome (1993), with its imposing and self-justifying title, *Veritatis Splendor* (*Splendour of Truth*), makes a positive answer seem most unlikely in the near future. But our ever-accelerating history may yet tell (as it has told before in the case of the many thousand years of ancient Egyptian 'certainties') that the institutions if not the originator 'got the message wrong'.

'Churchianity' has failed us. In George Steiner's phrase at his 1994 Salzburg lecture, 'The churches flounder in mundane compromise and theological vacancy.' They have mostly left us trying to deal on our own with a new Dark Age, and it is about time to question all the 'facts' and the myths and the historical jugglings anew. The slate needs wiping clean so that we can re-start from where we are. Some are already doing it, of course, and not surprisingly, they are often women. Karen Armstrong, mentioned earlier, took the Pope to task in an hour-long TV programme for seeming to ignore the agonies perpetuated by his insistent ban on contraception, especially in the Third World ravaged by AIDS. Irish women, she observed, often now make their own decision. Tasleema Nasreen, the Bangladeshi writer, also questions infallibility of text and the male Ayatollahs who enforce it. In fighting for the rights of subjected Muslim women, she has created as much controversy and danger for herself as in the notorious case of Salman Rushdie. There will be many more examples, less highlighted by publicity, as women continue to establish their equality, world-wide.

Wiping the slate clean of accrued and encrusted theology has its attraction, of course, but the image is probably too precipitate and mere wishful-thinking. There is nothing quite so conservative and deep-rooted as religion. It takes a very long time to change, leave alone die out. But over the countless generations and years, change it will, and probably die to be born again. If Matthew Arnold's image for the dying of the sea of faith was on *Dover Beach*, then an image for religions that refuse to change and adapt with the times might be Shelley's 'Ozymandias, King of Kings' whose gigantic statue, discovered by 'a traveller in an antique land', lies broken in the desert:

'Look on my works, ye Mighty, and despair!'
Nothing beside remains. Round the decay
Of that colossal wreck, boundless and bare,
The lone and level sands stretch far away.

Turning from the dark side to the light again, another Friend[20] found that Janet Scott had expressed all the theology that was needed when she wrote: 'We may be Christian, Buddhist, Hindu - the Spirit seeks us and loves us, and calls us to turn to the universal love and unity. ...The Kingdom of God is present in every loving heart and selfless act.'[21] That is admirably uncomplicated. Although even here, there will be some who find difficulty over the word 'Kingdom' with its sexist overtone; or perhaps because it has been used recently by Don Cupitt in its Old Testament sense of a 'Kingdom-religion' which aims 'to integrate the human into the world, and vice versa'[22]; not to mention because of its really threatening and dismaying use by Middle American Christian fundamentalists. Moreover, quoting Janet Scott's eulogy to the Spirit that unites the principal faiths should not be taken to imply that Quaker Universalism is simply another form of inter-faith dialogue, although it is true that the latter will incline those who partake in it to a universalist viewpoint. Nor does it imply, as we said earlier, the syncretism of trying to unify the different traditions, although universal Love might well lead to such a consummation.

Quaker Universalism at this time stands, rather, for the recognition of what John Punshon terms an 'underlying psychic unity' which is evident in 'the functions and outward forms of all religions.' Punshon's words come from a 'Background Paper on *Universalism in the Quaker Tradition*'[23] in which he inclines to marginalise it as an interesting historical bywater of Quakerism. The QUG, on the other hand, sees the universalist approach as becoming the energy of the main flood. The principal component of youthful or early Quakerism is usually seen as the 'one Jesus' who spoke to George Fox's condition. But for others, the individual Inward Light, and that component of universalism inherent in mystical Christianity as elsewhere, has grown in this century to be at the heart of what might be termed later Quakerism.

6 No final revelation nor monopoly of truth

Truth is not divisible, with some parts being more true than others. One expression of the truth in culture or time may be preferred to another, but it is not thereby better, or more true in its truthfulness. It is merely different. Before he was even a Quaker, Isaac Penington had put it immortally in 1653: '...every Truth is true in its kind. It is substance in its own place, though it be but a shadow in another place (for it is but a reflection from an intenser substance), and the shadow is a true shadow, as the substance is a true substance.' From this it follows that all human souls are precious, whatever the shortcomings and betrayals in their expression; just as all Nature is beautiful and precious, whatever its perceived savagery or ugliness.

The assertion that there can be no final revelation nor monopoly of truth - as Quaker Universalists claim - does not deny the enormous value and glory of the different great prophets and teachers. We live in a plural universe, and its plurality has to be recognized alongside the distinctive existence of individual forms. Above all forms is the Logos, the creative energy at the heart of matter, indecipherable, mysterious, awe-inspiring, and ultimately unknowable by thought.

We saw the rite of passage for Anthony Freeman at Leicester repeated later at his church door: a case of nature imitating art (*pace* Wilde). A living theology is really an art-form, a matter of creative energy and process; and it is to be hoped that Quaker Universalists, having stated their position, at least for now, might move their practice in the direction of the arts. Painting, poetry, music and drama, can all contain universal themes and symbology. But the really important artefact is that of our own lives. As with Quakers everywhere, it is not our peculiar ways but our actions which speak for us. But Quaker or not, wherever we are born, to whatever culture, at whatever living standard, it is ourselves that we have to learn to know and control in the School of Being - that School in which we are all, in the final analysis, seekers after truth. Not after Truth with a capital 'T', for that we can never know in this life, but at least truth as far as it can be known in human space and time. The School of Being is in the business of turning mere ideas and thoughts of the spiritual life into the actions of day-by-day reality. The scenario that is required of us to play is one of heightened awareness, whereby 'meaning' and 'values' are made manifest. It is a precious scenario whose final significance, whatever the evils and miseries and deceits surrounding it, will proclaim the revelation shown to Mother Julian that '... all will be well'.

Early Friends had a vision of a universal community - God's humanity - drawn together by a recognition of the Inward Light that is everyone's birthright. They called themselves 'Children of Light'. In today's materialist darkness, the time is ripe once again for a similar fresh start that recognizes the unifying ground of individual spiritual enlightenment when it can find communal expression. There exists a real sense in the world today that our very survival may depend upon re-establishing that consensus of the heart which is non-intellectual, which does not rely on either education or culture, but only on the common humanity of blood and feeling. This is Jung's 'bond of an affective nature'. Such a sense is sometimes touched in an Olympic ceremony, or by the sight of the world's misery on television, especially of injured or starving children, when there is a shared public sense of the need, and of the mutual responsibility.

This consensus of the heart has no prescribed texts, no exclusive scripture; and although it may call upon all the wisdom, the poetry and insight that the human race has accumulated down the ages, it will do so not in an eclectic fashion, and certainly not in one of contentious rivalry, but as an honest seeking after 'new light from whatever quarter it may come'. It is in providing a forum for such an ongoing search, as was said earlier, that the Quaker Universalists have such a vital contribution to make. More seriously still, they may provide a springboard for both individual and corporate action. They answer the needs of a contemporary yearning which apprehends the One Spirit in the many guises, and however diverse in cultural thinking, is of one heart and one mind in recognizing the fearful necessity to act upon ideals, exercising what has been profoundly termed 'the special responsibility of those whom would dwell in love'.[24]

The greatest achievement is correct being. Most religions would probably agree on that; which makes a small start from the personal to the universal and back again. The Zen monk who creates his formal garden out of rocks and pebbles and rhythms, and then sits in front of its beauty, is making that circular journey. It seems that religion, like beauty, is in the eye of the beholder. But however diverse the culture and its spiritual expression, what is seen to be beautiful in all the manifold forms of nature - like the awe and majesty in the universal image of a rainbow - speaks of God's mysterious covenant with all the human race. We are one race, one people, a part of the whole conundrum of Creation, and in this there is a singular comfort and glory.

Notes and references

1 Ralph Hetherington. *Universalism and Spirituality*, Pendle Hill Publications, 1993, pages 28-29.

2 Rex Ambler, *The End of Words: issues in contemporary Quaker theology*, QHS, 1994. I am very grateful to the author for a pre-publication sight of his manuscript.

3 *The Independent*, 3 August, 1994.

4 Grace Blindell, QUG Committee.

5 Matthew Fox, The *Coming of the Cosmic Christ*, Harper and Row, 1988, page 50.

6 Ewert H. Cousins, *Christ of the 21st Century*, Element, 1992. The author is Director of The Center for Contemporary Spirituality in New York.

7 Jean Hardy, QUG Committee, whose Turvey paper inspired all of this paragraph.

8 Karen Armstrong. *A History of God*, Heinemann, 1993; Mandarin Paperbacks, 1994, page 457.

9 Rex Ambler, op.cit.

10 Lois Jenkin, QUG Committee.

11 David Jenkin, QUG Committee.

12 Norman Richardson, QUG Committee.

13 *Ibid*

14 Daniel A. Seeger, *'Universalist Spirituality'* in *Quaker Religious Thought*, No. 72, Greensboro, NC, USA., page 32.

15 Lorna Marsden, *The Universality of the Image*, QUG Pamphlet Series, No 9.

16 Professor John Hick in *The Independent*, 9th August, 1994.

17 Norman Richardson.

18 C G Jung, *The Undiscovered Self*, Routlege Kegan Paul, 1958, pages 96-106.

19 Graham Walker, QUG Committee. Graham died in 1993, and for all the 'toughness' of his comment, he was the gentlest of men.

20 Vi Walker, QUG Committee.

21 Janet Scott. *What Canst Thou Say?: Towards a Quaker theology*, Swarthmore Lecture, QHS, 1980.

22 Don Cupitt, *After All: religion without alienation*, SCM, 1994, page 117.

23 John Punshon, *Universalism in the Quaker Tradition*, phase 3, unit 1, background paper 3, in the 'Gifts and Discoveries' pack, published by Woodbrooke College, 1991.

24 Daniel A. Seeger, op.cit.